KEEP CALM AND TEACH ON

Strategies, Techniques, Tips, and Quotes for 21st Century Educators

GLORIA MARIE PELCHER

Copyright © 2013 Gloria Marie Pelcher

All rights reserved. No portion of this book may be used or reproduced in any manner whatsoever without written permission of the author or Creative Bluebird except in the case of brief quotations embodied in critical articles and reviews.

KEEP CALM AND TEACH ON
Strategies, Techniques, Tips, and Quotes for 21st Century Educators

ISBN-13: 978-0615819297
ISBN-10: 061581929X

Creative Bluebird
www.creativebluebird.com

Cover Design: GLORIA MARIE PELCHER

For book inquiries please visit
creativebluebird.com/contact

To every educator who goes above and
beyond day in and day out!

Contents

1	Introduction	1
2	Relationships	3
3	Organization	29
4	Classroom Management	55
5	25 Additional Tips	81
6	Notes	107
7	About The Author	109

Introduction

This book is dedicated to all the educators in the world! THANKS for your dedication, your commitment, and your courage. I know what it is like to have the great responsibility of educating the future because I am an educator myself!

I have been an educator for over 5 years. I love interacting with students and helping them explore their world. I learned early on that in order to succeed in the classroom you must come with a plan to accomplish all the demands that come along with being a teacher. Winging it really doesn't work that well in the classroom, unless you want to go home every day exhausted and frustrated.

As an educator you wear many hats (nurturer, nurse, counselor, etc.), you deal with many personalities (administrators, colleagues, parents, students), and let's not even start on all the paperwork! At times it can become all overwhelming!

It doesn't matter if you've been teaching for a very long time (so long you are now teaching kids that belong to your first students) or if you are new to the profession experiencing your first classroom and your first set of students THIS BOOK IS FOR YOU! I hope it inspires you to keep calm and teach on!

Gloria Marie Pelcher

KEEP CALM

Relationships

To be successful in any career requires great relationships. We are all in this together, and the health of your relationships can make or break your career.

Love kids, especially your students: Teach and demonstrate love to your students. This will help you get through tough days and help you display patience when patience is needed. In a room full of 20 + students there is bound to be conflict between students and between you and your students. Let love guide all of your conflict resolution. Your students will be able to feel your compassion for them, and will respond in a positive way.

A teacher affects eternity; he can never tell where his influence stops.
Henry Adams

Learn your students' passions and interests: We are all born with passions and things that excite us! These passions can be evident even at a very young age. As an adult, and especially as a teacher, there is a responsibility to foster the growth of the next generation. I once had a student who was obsessed with folding paper and so I introduced him to the art of origami and showed him a documentary on origami artists and he started bringing me these amazing pieces of artwork! It was really cool to see his paper folding skills develop.

Teach the children so that it will not be necessary to teach the adults.
Abraham Lincoln

Earn their heart and you have their mind: Each year your first job as a teacher is to build a relationship with your students. If they don't feel like you are interested in them and who they are they will not give you the time of day to teach them anything.

Ask yourself: 'Do I feel the need to laminate?' Then teaching is for you.
Gordon Korman

Share and connect with other teachers: Learn something new? Discovered a new website? Share with other teachers. When you share with others they become more apt to share with you. Don't be afraid to ask other teachers questions about how they teach and organize their classrooms. As teachers we are all in this together for the benefit of students. There is no need to hoard information or techniques. That's one of the reasons why I wrote this book! Connecting and sharing with your colleagues will make you into a better teacher.

He who opens a school door, closes a prison.
Victor Hugo

Share who you are: On the first day of school share with your students who you are by sharing your story and why you became an educator. Share your personal teaching mission statement. Don't have one? Create one (see page 107). You only get one chance to make a first impression so make it count!

The best teacher is the one who suggests rather than dogmatizes, and inspires his listener with the wish to teach himself.
Edward Bulwer-Lytton

Be a team player: See yourself as part of the learning community which is your school. Share your time and talents beyond just what is expected of you. As a teacher I see myself as part of a village, and all the students are part of my responsibility.

Genius without education is like silver in the mine.
Benjamin Franklin

Listen to your students: I call them "one time" stories, and they are endless. Stories about their parents, their aunts, their uncles, their grandparents, their siblings, their friends, their dogs, and their cats! The stories are sometimes short, but oh sometimes they are long. Very long. But listen. Listen to your students. You never know, they could have no one else in their lives willing to listen to them.

A master can tell you what he expects of you. A teacher, though awakens your own expectations.
Patricia Neal

Allow your students to get to know each other: Noise can be a scary thing inside a classroom so a lot of teachers just try to keep their class quiet. Inside my classroom there is noise, but there is respect for silence. I allow students to interact with each other. Peer teaching, project based learning, learning centers, games, etc. are ways to get your students interacting with each other. Through interaction they will get to know each other and respect for others grow when people have the opportunity to get to know each other.

To teach is to learn twice.
Joseph Joubert

Encourage self-advocacy: It's a tough world out there, and one of the greatest things you can instill in your students is self-advocacy. Teach your students to take responsibility for their learning, and to speak up when they don't understand or isn't receiving what they need. Teach them to stand up for themselves and believe in themselves as they navigate their educational journey. Children are smart, and capable of knowing what they need to succeed.

Who dares to teach must never cease to learn.
John C. Dana

Build relationships in the community: Write letters to local businesses and organizations, introduce your class to your community. Many businesses and organizations are willing to partner with classrooms, and when they do don't forget to send thank you letters.

When you teach your son, you teach your son's son.
    The Talmud

Use books to teach about relationships: There are many teachable books on the market that can help you teach your students about character and relationships. For example, *Slugs in Love* is an adorable book about love. Yes, kids will squirm at the name but the message is sweet.

The true teacher defends his pupils against his own personal influences...
Amos Alcott

Be open to parents: Parents can be your biggest ally or your biggest enemy. Of course you want them as your ally! Keep the communication between you and your students' parents open, think of the relationship as a partnership. In the first semester schedule to have a teacher-parent conference. This is an opportunity beyond "meet the teacher" night to establish a relationship with your parents. This is the time to communicate with your parents your expectations of what you expect from them and their student, and what they can expect from you.

Teachers open the door. You enter by yourself.
Chinese Proverb

Attend school functions: After a long day at work who wants to spend more time at the workplace? Really, no one! I am not suggesting you attend ALL school functions but do make it a point to go to some. When parents and students see teachers involved in school events it shows that the teachers care about the learning community.

Teaching should be full of ideas instead of stuffed with facts.
Author Unknown

Educate parents: The more parents understand what their students are learning in class the more they will feel that they can actually help their students. When I taught kindergarten I educated parents on the steps of reading and it really helped my students in the end. Get parents in the know and they will become better partners in the education of their students.

None of us got where we are solely by pulling ourselves up by our bootstraps. We got here because somebody - a parent, a teacher, an Ivy League crony or a few nuns - bent down and helped us pick up our boots.
Thurgood Marshall

Students are not their parents: Sometimes parents are not your biggest fan, they can get nasty and belligerent, but never treat the offspring unfairly just because the parents are misbehaving or because of a disagreement. Never make a student pay for their parents' transgressions.

The art of teaching is the art of assisting discovery.
Mark van Doren

Say it nicely: Conferences with parents can get tricky. How do you let a parent know their student talk too much without actually saying, "your student talks too much." Find euphemisms to help parents know exactly what is going on with their student. Talkative student? Say the student has the gift of gab. Overly active? Say the student has a lot of energy. Find ways to soften the blow of whatever the reality might be.

Teachers, I believe, are the most responsible and important members of society because their professional efforts affect the fate of the earth.
Helen Caldicott

Connect with other classrooms: Don't let your classroom become an island! There are many ways to connect with other classes. I often use Reader's Theater in my classroom and take the show on the road to other classes. The students love it (and it helps with their fluency!) and they get to connect with other classes. When I taught kindergarten my class would compete with the other kindergarten classes on how well they knew their letters and sounds as a class. We had a blast! Connecting with other classes builds campus wide comrade, and allow students to display leadership to lower grades and see where they are headed with higher grades.

Information is the currency of democracy.
Ralph Nader

Be careful with emails: Keep emails short and sweet. It is easy to come off the wrong way through text, the receiver has nothing to go on but the written words. There are no facial expression or tone of voice to gage the writer's intent. Also, remember that once you press send you can't take it back and that email could be used as "evidence". On the other hand, not all evidence is bad. Email is a good documentation.

The dream begins, most of the time, with a teacher who believes in you, who tugs and pushes and leads you on to the next plateau, sometimes poking you with a sharp stick called truth.
Dan Rather

Accept invitations: When students invite you to their events try your best to make the event. I've been to dance recitals, soccer games, and church functions in support of students. The more you support your students the more they will respect you as a teacher.

Teachers teach because they care. Teaching young people is what they do best. It requires long hours, patience, and care.
Horace Mann

Be nice to the secretary: School secretaries work on the front line, they interact with just about everyone. Show appreciation and respect to the secretary, you never know when you might need the secretary on your side.

The mediocre teacher tells. The good teacher explains. The superior teacher demonstrates. The great teacher inspires.
William Arthur Ward

Learn the developmental stage of your students: Developmental stages can come in handy when interacting with students. It is unreasonable to expect a certain behavior or skill from a student when they haven't even reached that developmental stage. Start with Piaget's Theory of Cognitive Development.

Anyone who stops learning is old, whether at twenty or eighty. Anyone who keeps learning stays young.
Henry Ford

Be true to your word: Be trustworthy with your students. If you say you are going to do something do it. If you promise your students an award follow through. If you promise your students a consequence follow through. Foster an healthy relationship with your students and the people around you by being true with your words.

One looks back with appreciation to the brilliant teachers, but with gratitude to those who touched our human feelings. The curriculum is so much necessary raw material, but warmth is the vital element for the growing plant and for the soul of the child.
Carl Jung

Exchange letters with students: When I get a letter from a student I write them back, and then the exchange of letters continue. Besides from building a relationship this also helps with their writing skills. These letters can be written in a notebook exchanged between teacher and student.

Education is light, lack of it darkness.
Russian Proverb

Invite parents: Some parents are more than willing to help out in the classroom. Invite parents to read to students, do prep work on activities, and take on organizational tasks. Take an all hands on deck approach.

In a completely rational society, the best of us would be teachers and the rest of us would have to settle for something less.
Lee Iacocca

Give thanks: Get a stack of Thank You cards and be ready to say thanks! Throughout your teaching career there will be many people who will do things for you and your students. Always show appreciation.

If you plan for a year, plant a seed. If for ten years, plant a tree. If for a hundred years, teach the people. When you sow a seed once, you will reap a single harvest. When you teach the people, you will reap a hundred harvests.
Kuan Chung

Organization

In the course of a school year you use a lot of materials and if you are self-contained you have even more things in your classroom. Instead of just piling stuff in your classroom stop and brainstorm about the best location for everything. You don't want to be known as the disorganized teacher.

Make charts, lots of them: Use charts to organize everything. The most common classroom chart is the job chart, but brainstorm more areas in the class that you can use a chart. Seeing data represented in charts in the classroom is a good way for students to see real life application of data being represented.

I like a teacher who gives you something to take home to think about besides homework.
Lily Tomlin as Edith Ann

Go paperless: Go paperless for at least one week! Use whiteboards, songs, group discussions, multimedia and visuals instead of any worksheets. Coincide this week near Earth Day.

When our students fail, we, as teachers, too, have failed.
Marva Collins

Organize papers: Have a place for all papers. Get a filing system in place before school even starts and stick with it. For example, I have baskets labeled homework, classwork, graded, needs grading, needs filing, etc. Paper should never float around on your desk.

There are three things to remember when teaching: know your stuff; know whom you are stuffing; and then stuff them elegantly.
Lola May

Organize copies: Create a system that allows you to know exactly what has been copied and what needs to be copied. Some teachers organize their copies in a Monday - Friday system and some organize their copies by subject. I use the by subject method because sometimes you may not get to a resource on the exact day that you planned.

The average teacher explains complexity; the gifted teacher reveals simplicity.
Robert Brault

Keep track of student's information: Each student should have their own file folder with important information in the file folder. Be ready for a meeting concerning any student at any time! I keep in the folder the student's profile that I have parents fill out at the beginning of the year, test scores, reading running records, sample work, any correspondents between me and the parent or student, behavior records, and any other important information. I also keep blank conference log sheets, literally ready for a conference at any time!

I'm not a teacher but an awakener.
Robert Frost

Go digital with worksheets and pintables: Instead of having an actual file cabinet of worksheets and activities replace books and worksheets with digital resources. Go through your teacher books and worksheets and find similar activities online that you can save as pdf or bookmark. However you would organize a file cabinet organize your digital files the same way. Invest in a portable hard drive or consider an online cloud drive.

A good teacher is like a candle – it consumes itself to light the way for others.
Author Unknown

Arrange classroom according to need: The flow of your classroom is important in creating the correct learning environment. How my classroom is set up at the beginning of the year is not how my classroom is at the end of the year. I believe in making adjustments according to the needs of my students.

The mind is not a vessel to be filled, but a fire to be ignited.
Plutarch

Label everything: This is good for helping kids with environmental print, but also to show students exactly where things belong. Labels also reinforce the concept that there is a place for everything. Download creative labels from teacherspayteachers.com.

The true aim of every one who aspires to be a teacher should be, not to impart his own opinions, but to kindle minds.
F. W. Robertson

Use binder rings: These are one of the best office supply inventions ever! Use ring binders to hold instructional routines, sight words, vocabulary words, and things that need rotating like names on the job chart and centers schedule (put all the student's names on index cards on the ring binder and rotate each week).

To know how to suggest is the great art of teaching.
Henri Frederic Amiel

Create student binders: At the beginning of the year I set each of my students up with a 3 ring binder to keep handouts organized. You can section the binder off into each of the main subjects. At the beginning of the year I tell my students that if I give them any paper (like reference handouts such as phonic charts) that has a 3 ring hole punch in it that I expect for them to put it in the binder.

You can pay people to teach, but you can't pay them to care.
Marva Collins

Have a teacher binder: In the last section of this book I talk about keeping a teacher journal, but for organizational purposes you should also have a teacher 3 ring binder. In my teacher binder I 3 ring hole punch any papers that I might need to refer back to. Most of these papers come from the front office or important information from the beginning of the year such as schedules, new procedures, login information for websites, etc. Besides from my teacher binder I also have a binder to document intervention. Binders are a great way to organize just about anything!

You can't direct the wind but you can adjust the sails.
Author Unknown

Use wall space: Where I teach space is a luxury and in small spaces you must become creative. Take advantage of wall space. Find a way to place things that normally go on a table on the wall. For example, instead of using a bucket of pencils on a table I use baskets hung on the wall for class pencils. To help with hanging things on the wall consider covering part of a wall with pegboard. I have also seen rain gutters being used to shelve books along the wall.

The teacher who is indeed wise does not bid you to enter the house of his wisdom but rather leads you to the threshold of your mind.
Kahlil Gibran

Create an information center: Instead of having the birthday chart, the job chart, class schedule, and other information spread out across the classroom create a central location where all this important information can be found.

The teachers who get "burned out" are not the ones who are constantly learning, which can be exhilarating, but those who feel they must stay in control and ahead of the students at all times. Frank Smith

Create a supply center: If you have communal supplies organize them neatly in one location with labeled baskets. House all glue, pens, markets, pencils, papers, staples, scissors, crayons, etc. in this one central location. Teach students how to handle supplies, including how to put them back in their proper place. If your classroom is set up in tables create ready to go caddies for each table, then the person responsible for getting the supplies can just pick up their table's caddy.

For every person who wants to teach there are approximately thirty people who don't want to learn much.
W.C. Stellar

Organize your classroom decorations: My first year of teaching I barely had any posters, borders, letters, or any type of decorations, but I quickly accumulated tons of stuff! It is worth investing in border and poster organizers.

Everything should be made as simple as possible, but not simpler.
Albert Einstein

Have books, but not too many: I know how much teachers love books, but they can really clutter the classroom. Since my first year of teaching I have had this one book rack that serves my classroom well, and it doesn't take up much space. Students often bring books from home to read in class, or if you have a school library students can use that resource as a bigger source of books.

Teaching is not a lost art, but the regard for it is a lost tradition.
Jacques Barzun

Repurpose items: Organizing can become expensive, but you can easily repurpose items into containers. A sanitizing wipe container can be used as a scissor caddy, a baby wipe container can be used to house crayons, sandwich bag boxes can be used to hold pencils, cereal boxes as filing boxes, and the list goes on. Need more ideas? Search pinterest.com!

The man (or woman) who can make hard things easy is the educator.
Ralph Waldo Emerson

Plan ahead: Part of being organized is planning ahead. If you don't plan ahead for anything else plan ahead with your lesson planning and copies. Instead of doing weekly lesson plans week by week try planning for multiple weeks at a time. Instead of being at the copy machine every morning take time during the previous week to make copies for the current week.

Children are like wet cement; whatever falls on them makes an impression.
Haim Ginott

Assign class numbers: Each student should be assigned a class number based on alphabetical order. Teach students the procedure of putting their name, date, AND class number on each paper. Besides from aiding in quickly filing papers having class numbers allows you to easily section off the class into groups if needed. You could call odd numbers, even numbers, two digit numbers, 1-5, etc.

The test of a good teacher is not how many questions he can ask his pupils that they will answer readily, but how many questions he inspires them to ask him which he finds it hard to answer.
Alice Wellington Rollins

Purge: I started my teaching career in 4th grade, I moved to 2nd grade, then I taught kindergarten for 2 years, and then I was moved back to 2nd grade. My accumulation of things "I might need someday" grew, and grew. At some point you just have to let it go, do a deep purge of things you are no longer using. If you are not using it then you don't need it. My wishful thinking dream is to have everything I need to teach in one box.

Teaching kids to count is fine, but teaching them what counts is best.
Bob Talbert

Have a work table: One way to keep your desk clean is to have a work table near your desk. Store your supplies and things you access daily on the table. This will keep your desk pristine! A clean desk allows you to breathe.

Education is not the filling of a pail, but the lighting of a fire.
William Butler Yeats

Make packets/booklets: Instead of having a lot of single pages flying free consider making weekly packets/booklets of worksheets and activities for each subject, and have students access the packets/booklets as needed. Also, consider making homework packets for the week. On Monday give students the homework packet for the whole week with the due date towards the end of the week.

If we teach today's students as we taught yesterday's, we rob them of tomorrow.
John Dewey

IF you take work home: Organize papers you take home in a portable expanding file folder, and keep everything neatly within that portable expanding file folder. This prevents stacks of papers from being in the backseat of your car, on the floor in your living room, and wherever else stacks of papers like to rest. Better yet, instead of taking it home team up with a fellow teacher and get the work done at a local coffee shop.

A child cannot be taught by anyone who despises him, and a child cannot afford to be fooled.
James Baldwin

Organize units: Throughout the year most curriculums cover materials in themed units. Consider the best way to organize the artifacts of these units, and make sure they are easily accessible year after year. I have seen some teachers use binders with zip pockets to put everything in (animal binder, weather binder, etc.), or some use labeled clear boxes/tubs.

Teaching is the one profession that creates all other professions.
Author Unknown

Don't overdo it: At the beginning of the year it is easy to get super excited and hang tons of stuff in your classroom. Leave a little of what is called white space on your wall, and room to display work from students.

Modern cynics and skeptics see no harm in paying those to whom they entrust the minds of their children a smaller wage than is paid to those to whom they entrust the care of their plumbing.
John F. Kennedy

Classroom Management

If your students are out of control there is no way to effectively teach. It is of utmost importance that you sharpen your classroom management skills.

Model good behavior: Students look up to you and watch your every move. Be a positive model for them. The way you talk to your students is most likely the way they will talk to each other within your classroom. If you have a bad disposition most likely your students will also have the same disposition. You set the tone for your classroom.

The important thing is not so much that every child should be taught, as that every child should be given the wish to learn.
John Lubbock

Have procedures for EVERYTHING: Never leave it up to the kids to figure out the best way to do something in the classroom. Students need procedures for everything. Don't leave it up to chance that they might quietly line up, return supplies to its proper place, request to go to the restroom politely and non-intrusively, and all the other things that take place in the classroom. The song "This is the Way We Clap Our Hands" comes to mind when talking about procedures. Show students how to move throughout the classroom and the day.

The whole purpose of education is to turn mirrors into windows.
Sydney J. Harris

Know the difference between a procedure and a rule: A rule is basically something that is not done and a procedure is how to do something that is done.

A teacher who is attempting to teach without inspiring the pupil with a desire to learn is hammering on cold iron.
Horace Mann

Set high expectations: Students are incredible beings; they will do incredible things IF there is an expectation for incredible things. Also, remember to play fair, and not favorites! It's easy to play favorites without even knowing it, but be aware of this. Apply the same academic and behavior expectations to all students, and make sure these expectations are set high.

If kids come to us from strong, healthy functioning families, it makes our job easier. If they do not come to us from strong, healthy, functioning families, it makes our job more important.
Barbara Colorose

Outlaw hitting: If you are going to make a big deal about anything this would be the thing to make a big deal about. From the onset of the school year you must outlaw physical aggressive behavior in your classroom. Everyone should feel safe in the classroom. Create a zero violence tolerance environment. Period. Some kids will be challenged by this policy if they are use to displaying aggressive behaviors at home, but overtime you can weed out such behaviors. Have a clear consequence for this type of behavior and always follow through.

Who dares to teach must never cease to learn.
John Cotton Dana

Be the adult: I love kids to death but they have no real idea of what is best for them, have you seen a kid after Halloween eat candy like it's the most nutritious thing ever? Their decision making skills are not quite developed. Most of them still believe in Santa Clause. They still need tons of guidance. This is where you come in. Maintain your adult role in all situations. Know your role.

Those who educate children well are more to be honored than they who produce them; for these only gave them life, those the art of living well.
Aristotle

Tame your students: *Where The Wild Things Are* is one of my favorite books. In the story the main character Max ends up where the wild things are, a bunch of unruly monsters, but Max eventually tames the wild things and crowns himself king. On the first day of school you are Max and your students are the wild things and it is your job to tame them and become ruler of your classroom. For 3 months out of a year most kids spend their time running wild and free, and most kids will continue to rock and roll the other 9 months of the year unless someone puts a stop to their party.

In learning you will teach, and in teaching you will learn.
Phil Collins

Be firm: A lot of teachers don't tame their students because they are afraid of being seen as the bad guy. Who wants to stop a party? Who wants to be seen as the fun killer? Or the rule enforcer, or the mean teacher? No one. But here is the deal, you won't be seen as a mean teacher, your students will actually appreciate the civility in your classroom. Many times I've had to put my foot down in a very firm way, of course it isn't a fun thing to do, but at the end of the day my students didn't hate me for it!

Every truth has four corners: as a teacher I give you one corner, and it is for you to find the other three.
Confucius

Never label kids: Avoid the temptation to label a student as "bad" or any other negative label because it could crush or deflate a student's feelings. Be sensitive to student's feelings and how you talk to them or about them.

It is not what is poured into a student that counts but what is planted.
Linda Conway

Say NO to yelling: Yelling accomplishes little. It is not an effective strategy to get your point across. Teach your students how to effectively communicate. Listen and respond in kindness. Besides, yelling is extremely tiring. Remember, the goal is to keep calm and teach on!

If a doctor, lawyer, or dentist had 40 people in his office at one time, all of whom had different needs, and some of whom didn't want to be there and were causing trouble, and the doctor, lawyer, or dentist, without assistance, had to treat them all with professional excellence for nine months, then he might have some conception of the classroom teacher's job.
Donald Quinn

Create and stick to a discipline plan: Your discipline plan should have what you expect from students and it should outline the consequences involved with students who do not abide by the expectations and the rewards for students who abide by the expectations. It should be a written document, not something you make up along the way. Discipline plans should be strictly adhered to EVERY SINGLE DAY. A nonnegotiable. The moment you start negotiating on your discipline plan will be the moment students will start making up their own plan. I am very familiar with my classroom discipline plan and this familiarity comes in handy when talking to students and parents.

An investment in knowledge pays the best interest.
Benjamin Franklin

Don't argue with students: Never argue with students over anything, especially well laid out expectations that they desire to break or bend. The best way to deal with students who want to argue is to show empathy but be repetitive in your response. For example, "I'm sorry but you are not allowed to do that." And when they continue, stick to your guns, "I'm sorry, I know how you want to do that but it's not allowed." And when they still persist? Simply tell them that you don't argue with students, then divert attention elsewhere.

It's not that I'm so smart, it's just that I stay with problems longer.
Albert Einstein

Let kids be kids: Let kids enjoy their youth. Allow them opportunities to laugh, play, dance, sing, and talk. These are all normal parts of being a kid. If you don't give students opportunities to do these things, to be who they are, they will steal the moments at inappropriate times.

The greatest sign of success for a teacher ... is to be able to say, 'The children are now working as if I did not exist.
Maria Montessori

Take brain breaks: Students can get antsy real quick. Take a break from it all, let them get up and move. Find fun videos and songs that allow students to get up and dance and sing, or do something silly like go on an imaginary bear hunt! The company Teach Train Love (teachtrainlove.com) has an awesome video collection for brain breaks.

You cannot teach a man anything; you can only help him find it within himself.
Galileo Galilei

Have community supplies: In lower grades community supplies are a perfect way to teach and build the concept of community. In the upper grades kids like having their own unique supplies, and that is perfectly fine. Allow kids to have their own supply box but also have some community supplies for everyone to use. For example, since pencils are the most popular school supply item have a set of "sharp" and "dull" pencils ready for students to use at all times. Don't waste instructional time discussing supplies.

Technology is just a tool. In terms of getting the kids working together and motivating them, the teacher is the most important.
Bill Gates

Deliver high quality content: Students get bored easily, we live in a world of short attention spans and information in society is delivered in a way that takes that into account. If you don't like how the content is delivered there are options, turn the channel, go to a different website, etc. Students come to school with this same mentality, if they are not engaged they will seek other options. Students are very creative with creating options in the classroom.

Teaching is not a lost art, but the regard for it is a lost tradition.
Jacques Barzun

See yourself as a coach: I am constantly aware of my student's behavior. My job is to coach them into better students, to motivate them to want to do the right thing. I often will say things like, "does that look educational?" or "does the classroom sound educational?" to my students. I constantly remind them how they are supposed to walk in the line (and model it!), how they are supposed to enter the classroom, etc.

I have come to believe that a great teacher is a great artist and that there are as few as there are any other great artists. Teaching might even be the greatest of the arts since the medium is the human mind and spirit.
John Steinbeck

Review expectations every day: After the morning pledge and the moment of silence my students go directly into reciting the classroom expectations in affirmation form. "I will listen carefully..." This give students a little friendly reminder of what is expected of them. Some days I will chime in and give extra "encouragement" to them about the day.

True teachers are those who use themselves as bridges over which they invite their students to cross; then, having facilitated their crossing, joyfully collapse, encouraging them to create their own.
Nikos Kazantzakis

Create permanent jobs: I tell my students that I need people who can get certain jobs done day in and day out. For example, not every student is cut out to be a restroom monitor. Let students "apply" for theses permanent jobs by writing a letter to you explaining why they will be a perfect fit for the job. This gives students an opportunity to practice a real life skill and it gives you a student who is perfect for the job.

Only those who look with the eyes of children can lose themselves in the object of their wonder.
Eberhard Arnold

Emphasize choices: I always tell my students that the choices they make today will affect their whole life, the big ones and the small ones. When I redirect behavior I often will say, "I need you to make a better choice" or ask them, "are you making good choices?" These type of statements and questions put the responsibility of good behavior on the student. As a teacher you can't force a student to make a good choice, but you can get them thinking about if what they are doing is a good choice or a bad choice.

Seek opportunities to show you care. The smallest gestures often make the biggest difference.
John Wooden

Have work for early finishers: In every class you will have those *zoom-zoom-done* kids, and you better have a plan for them for when they are done. I normally give students each a folder that they keep at their desk or table, and in that folder there are always things for them to do whether it is unfinished work or skill builders (cursive practice, math drills, etc.). A key part in classroom management is to keep kids busy, busy, busy!

When you study great teachers... you will learn much more from their caring and hard work than from their style.
William Glasser

Conduct classroom meetings: Every now and then conduct classroom meetings, an open forum for students' voices to be heard. Listen to what your students tell you, and improve your classroom's environment. Students will appreciate the fact that you care enough to take into account their ideas and suggestions. You'll be surprised at the level of insight of your students. This is also a good time to voice your concerns about the classroom and to reiterate classroom expectations. Keep the mood of the classroom meeting positive, and it will be well worth the time.

We never know which lives we influence, or when, or why.
Stephen King

Morning work: This is also known as bell ringers. Some schools allow students in the classroom before the first bell of the day and students should be on task from the start of the day. Always have something ready for them, preferably the same type of work every morning. This is a good time for kids to practice their facts or handwriting. Mundane? Perhaps! However, it will set the tone of structure for the rest of the day.

Real learning comes about when the competitive spirit has ceased.
Jiddu Krishnamurti

If you are disappointed in behavior make it known: Most students love to please, and hate when people they look up to are disappointed in them. If my class is behaving incorrectly I will make it known to them that I am disappointed in them. I will tell them things like, "I am really disappointed that you all are choosing to run in the hallway."

We now understand that higher-level thinking is more likely to occur in the brain of a student who is emotionally secure than in the brain of a student who is scared, upset, anxious, or stressed.
Mawhinney and Sagan

Thank and praise students when they are doing well: It's so easy to go through your day just redirecting students and not really praising them when they are doing well. Students will respond to praise by doing more of the things that will get them more praise. Make it a point to thank your students for lining up quietly, being helpful, being on task, etc. Be specific with the praise. For example, "thank you for lining up with your hands behind your back and a bubble in your mouth."

To know how to suggest is the art of teaching.
Henri-Frédéric Amiel

25
Additional Tips

See yourself as a problem solver! No matter what comes your way throughout the year or throughout the day know that you are capable of handling it. The work that you do as an educator is life changing and ultimately world changing. You are a professional. Keep up the good work!

Know why you are a teacher: Why are you a teacher? Know the answer to this question. When you know your purpose things make more sense.

There's a lot of talk these days about giving children self-esteem. It's not something you can give; it's something they have to build. Coach Graham worked in a no-coddling zone. Self-esteem? He knew there was really only one way to teach kids how to develop it: You give them something they can't do, they work hard until they find they can do it, and you just keep repeating the process."
Randy Pausch

Become a lifelong learner: Teaching is a transfer of understanding and knowledge. The more you know the more your students will know. Never stop learning! Seek out opportunities to deepen your knowledge of how things work in the world, and seek out professional development that will enhance your professional skills (books, workshops, blogs, newsletters, magazines, etc.).

When you wish to instruct, be brief; that men's [children's] minds take in quickly what you say, learn its lesson, and retain it faithfully. Every word that is unnecessary only pours over the side of a brimming mind.
Marcus Tullius Cicero

Play games: Think of ways to learn through games. Students love playing games and being competitive, and they are pretty good at making up games as well. Heads up, they are going to want a prize for winning!

His older self had taught his younger self a language which the older self knew because the younger self, after being taught, grew up to be the older self and was, therefore, capable of teaching."
Robert A. Heinlein

Play music: Any opportunity you get to play music in the classroom seize it. I start every day off in my classroom with music! Music can put kids into a positive attitude and activate brain waves. Also, there are tons of educational music available for learning multiplication facts, grammar, and other educational knowledge. Music is also beneficial to ELL students. Amazon.com has a wide selection of free children's music.

Teaching is only demonstrating that it is possible.
Learning is making it possible for yourself.
Paulo Coelho

Observe other teachers: Study and learn best practices by observing other teachers. You can learn from veteran teachers and new teachers alike. Don't have time to observe teachers on your campus? No problem, there are tons of videos of teachers teaching online. One of my favorites is learner.org.

In a completely rational society, the best of us would be teachers and the rest of us would have to settle for something else.
Lee Iacocca

Use composition notebooks: Love these! There are so many uses for them in the classroom. They can be used in all the subjects in a variety of ways. I like them better than spirals because the binding is stronger. Composition books can be cut in half at your local hardware store and made into little composition books.

If you think education is expensive, try ignorance.
Andy McIntyre

Keep a teacher journal: Besides from students using composition books I also use one as my teacher journal. Instead of having tons of notes everywhere I use my teacher journal to write down notes and reminders and to take notes during meetings.

Without language, one cannot talk to people and understand them; one cannot share their hopes and aspirations, grasp their history, appreciate their poetry, or savor their songs.
Nelson Mandela

Know the what and how of your state standards: Print out your state standards and know them, once you know the standards have a plan on how to teach them. This will help in making sure your students are getting everything they need to be successful for the next grade level. Many concepts build from grade to grade, make sure you cover all your basis. Also, post standards in your classroom so students will always know their objective. Most states have adopted the Common Core Standards and they can be found at corestandards.org.

Share your knowledge. It is a way to achieve immortality.
Dalai Lama XIV

Include movement and communication: Incorporate as many activities as you can into your lessons that allow students to move and share with their peers, this will cut down on unwanted movement and communication in your classroom.

Teachers have three loves: love of learning, love of learners, and the love of bringing the first two loves together.
Scott Hayden

Chunk information: In the section on delivering high quality content I talked about short attention spans and another way to deal with short attention spans is by chunking information. For example, consider presenting information in bulleted points, 2-3 steps, groupings, flow charts, or numbered lists. After around 10 minutes of absorbing information the brain will often zone out.

A teacher who cannot explain any abstract subject to a child does not himself thoroughly understand his subject; if he does not attempt to break down his knowledge to fit the child's mind, he does not understand teaching.
Fulton J. Sheen

Use visual aids for everything: We live in a visual society, images are everywhere! Support instruction with visual aids. If you have a way to present PowerPoint presentations get good at making presentations to present to your students. If you have no access to visual aids draw it! Even if you think you draw terribly still draw it! Students won't mind at all your stick figures! Also you can find a huge collection of photos at images.google.com.

Proper teaching is recognized with ease. You can know it without fail because it awakens within you that sensation which tells you this is something you have always known.
Frank Herbert

Know your abbreviations: As a new teacher abbreviations can make things confusing! Get a good grasp on all the educational abbreviations that are commonly used within education amongst colleagues.

Start by doing what's necessary, then what's possible, and suddenly you are doing the impossible.
St. Francis of Assisi

Get an educator's calendar: Do you know when Dr. Suess birthday is? Do you know when Earth Day is? If you are a teacher you should know these type of dates! Use an educator's calendar to stay in the know on fun holidays that can lead into valuable learning opportunities. You can download one at teachervision.com.

Learning to read is probably the most difficult and revolutionary thing that happens to the human brain and if you don't believe that, watch an illiterate adult try to do it.
John Steinbeck

Be excited about teaching: Be excited about teaching and your students will be excited about learning. Excitement is contagious! If you are ho-hum don't expect students to be eager to learn.

For the advice in a joke is sometimes more useful than the most serious teaching.
Balthasar Gracian

Document EVERYTHING: Sometimes you will find yourself in situations where your word is not good enough, in situations where you need proof! Always create a paper trail. Always. Document everything! Document interventions you give, document behavior, document conversations, etc. Keep all graded papers until the dust settles from report cards. Pen and paper never forgets. Consider buying carbon copy paper from the office supply store for those times you don't have time to type up a letter or make a copy of the letter.

I'm not a teacher: only a fellow traveler of whom you asked the way. I pointed ahead - ahead of myself as well as you."
George Bernard Shaw

Learn the copy machine: Unless you have a personal assistant you will make thousands of copies over your lifespan as a teacher. Most copy machines have the same features and functions, learn these features and functions to expedite your time in front of the copy machine and to better create copies exactly how you want them. I see so many teachers hand stapling documents when most copy machines will staple your documents for you.

The fundamental purpose of school is learning, not teaching.
Richard DuFour

Find your inner Anne Sullivan: Anne Sullivan was Helen Keller's teacher, and you might find yourself with a student who seems impossible but know that every student can learn. Stay at the black well and don't be quick to throw in the towel when a student is having a difficult time grasping a concept.

In God's eyes, a man who teaches one truth and nothing else is more righteous than a man who teaches a million truths and one lie.
Criss Jami

Use "I do, we do, you do": Previously I mentioned modeling good behavior for your students, but modeling comes in handy in all areas of being a good teacher. When you use "I do, we do, you do" the first step is modeling the concept, the next step is guided practice, then allow the student to practice mastering the skill. Don't expect students to know if you don't first show.

The best way to learn is to do; the worst way to teach is to talk.
Paul Halmos

See yourself as a reading teacher: No matter what subject or grade level you teach see yourself as a reading teacher. You will have students come to you with gaps in their reading knowledge and it would be beneficial for you to have a good grasp on the fundamentals of reading.

If you want to teach people a new way of thinking, don't bother trying to teach them. Instead, give them a tool, the use of which will lead to new ways of thinking.
Richard Buckminster Fuller

Learn how to create materials: Sometimes what you need you just don't have or can't find, and in these cases make it! Learn how to use computer software that enables you to create materials.

I have always had the greatest respect for students. There is nothing I hate more than condescension—the attitude that they are inferior to you. I always assume they have good minds."
Mark Van Doren

Down to a science: There are some things that there is no need to mix up every day or every week! I've talked about morning work already, but it is one of those things you should have down to a science. Each day you shouldn't have to think about what your students will do when they enter into the classroom. Homework is another area that you should have down to a science! Get a good system for meaningful homework in place and stick to it. Some things you can put on autopilot!

The difference between a beginning teacher and an experienced one is that the beginning teacher asks, "How am I doing?" and the experienced teacher asks, "How are the children doing?"
Esm

Let the students become teachers: Students love role playing. Give them opportunities to play teacher! If my class is working on a challenging concept halfway through the class period I will ask students who feel like they can teach the concept to raise their hands, and after I identify the "teachers" I instruct the "students" who are still struggling with the concept to go find a teacher. You are no longer the only teacher in the classroom, and this is a win-win for everyone. Peer to peer instruction is a very effective classroom strategy in getting students at the mastery level in any concept.

It's not that I'm so smart, it's just that I stay with problems longer.
Albert Einstein

Be aware of learning styles: There is a lot of talk about Differentiated Instruction in the classroom, and a good place to start with DI is knowing the learning styles of your students and being aware of the different ways information acquisition takes place. The most common and widely-used categorization of learning styles come from Neil Fleming and they include visual learners, auditory learners, kinesthetic learners, and tactile learners.

Start by doing what's necessary, then what's possible, and suddenly you are doing the impossible.
St. Francis of Assisi

Save your voice: Students will respond to gestures and sounds, as much as your voice. Therefore, save your voice and implement gestures and sounds into your classroom. You could use a bell instead of your voice to get students' attention. I have also seen teachers clap in a rhythm to gain the attention of their class. The important thing here is that you should have a method of getting your class' attention without having to talk over the noise and a method that works!

Teaching is the highest form of understanding.
Aristotle

Have a substitute folder: I started my teaching career as a substitute teacher and I was always thankful when the absent teacher had a plan in place in case of a planned or unplanned absence. Besides, you owe it to your students to keep some kind of normalcy going while you are away. Your sub folder (or tub) should have at least your lesson plans, class roster, schedules, any allergy notes concerning students, explanation of your behavior plan, specific behavior issues, how to use any special electronic devices, and activities for students to do. At the least.

No one learns as much about a subject as one who is forced to teach it.
Peter F. Drucker

My Teaching Mission Statement

_____
_____
_____
_____
_____
_____
_____
_____
_____
_____

Notes

About Gloria Marie Pelcher

GLORIA MARIE PELCHER lives in Dallas, TX. She has been an educator for over 5 years. She has published multiple books and blogs regularly at gloriamarie.com. Her mission is to inspire you to DREAM & live your purpose!™

Get More!

keepcalmandteachon.com

Connect!

gloriamarie.com
twitter.com/gloriamarie
facebook.com/gloriamarie

If you are interested in having Gloria Marie Pelcher at your next event visit gloriamarie.com/events

KEEP CALM

AND TEACH ON! :)

www.ingramcontent.com/pod-product-compliance
Lightning Source LLC
Chambersburg PA
CBHW032140040426
42449CB00005B/340